BRAVE JANE AUSTEN

READER, WRITER, AUTHOR, REBEL

LISA PLISCOU

Illustrated by
JEN CORACE

Christy Ottaviano Books

HENRY HOLT AND COMPANY · NEW YORK

With warmest thanks to Laura Ross, Steve Wineman,
Cheryl Pientka, Christy Ottaviano, and Sarah Emsley:
—L. P.

"My idea of good company . . . is the company of clever, well-informed people,
who have a great deal of conversation; that is what I call good company."

"You are mistaken," said he gently, "that is not good company; that is the best."

—Jane Austen, *Persuasion*

Henry Holt and Company, *Publishers since 1866*
Henry Holt® is a registered trademark of Macmillan Publishing Group, LLC
175 Fifth Avenue, New York, NY 10010 · mackids.com

We extend our gratitude to the Blair Partnership for confirming
J. K. Rowling's quote about Jane Austen included in this book.

Library of Congress Cataloging-in-Publication Data
Names: Pliscou, Lisa author. | Corace, Jen illustrator.
Title: Brave Jane Austen : reader, writer, author, rebel / by Lisa Pliscou ; illustrated by Jen Corace.
Description: First edition. | New York : Christy Ottaviano Books, Henry Holt and Company, 2018.
Identifiers: LCCN 2017021039 | ISBN 9781627796439 (hardcover)
Subjects: LCSH: Austen, Jane, 1775–1817—Juvenile literature. | Novelists, English—19th century—Biography—Juvenile literature.
Classification: LCC PR4036 .P55 2017 | DDC 823/.7 [B]—dc23
LC record available at https://lccn.loc.gov/2017021039

Our books may be purchased in bulk for promotional, educational, or business use.
Please contact your local bookseller or the Macmillan Corporate and Premium Sales Department
at (800) 221-7945 ext. 5442 or by e-mail at MacmillanSpecialMarkets@macmillan.com.

First edition, 2018 / Designed by April Ward
The artist used gouache, ink, acrylic, and pencil on Rives BFK paper.
Printed in China by RR Donnelley Asia Printing Solutions Ltd., Dongguan City, Guangdong Province
1 3 5 7 9 10 8 6 4 2

For my father, who with his steadfast love
has encouraged me all my life
—L. P.

For Iris Naomi
—J. C.

A long time ago, in a tiny village in England,
there was a little girl named Jane.
There was no reason to think she would grow up
to be anything out of the ordinary.

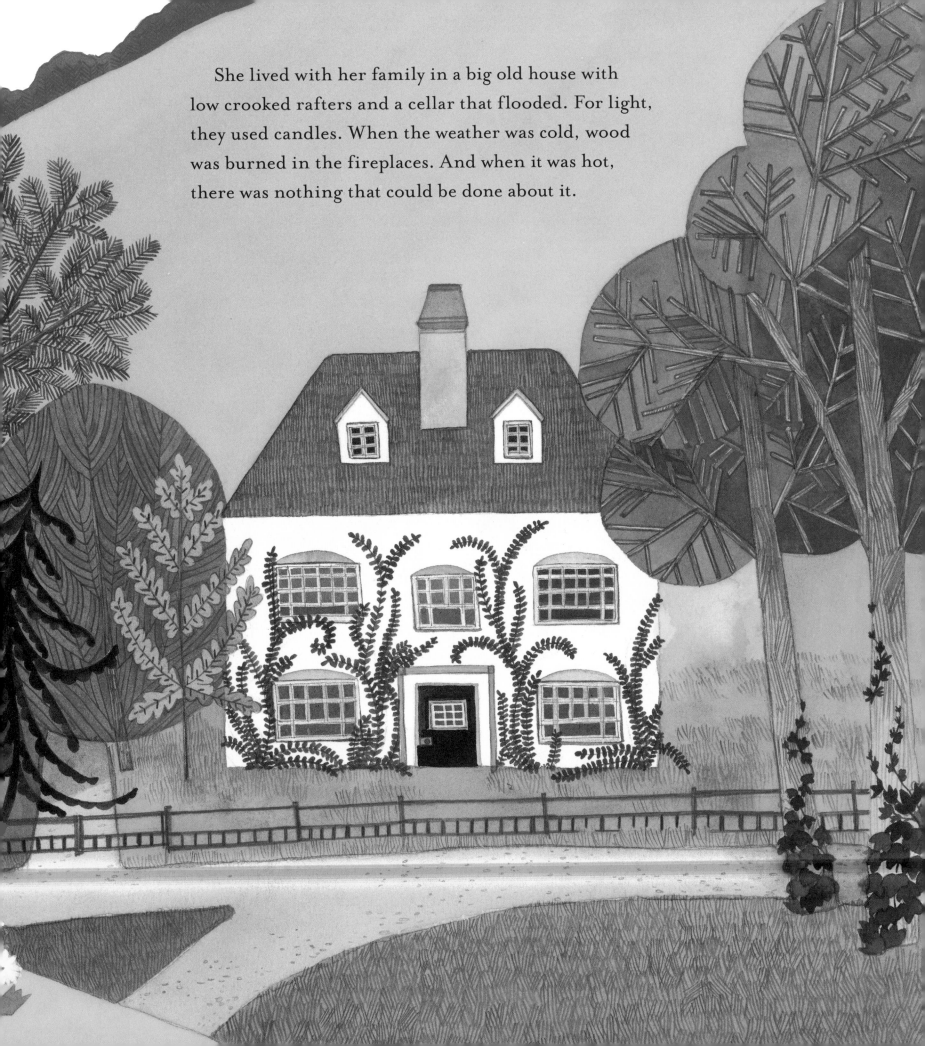

She lived with her family in a big old house with low crooked rafters and a cellar that flooded. For light, they used candles. When the weather was cold, wood was burned in the fireplaces. And when it was hot, there was nothing that could be done about it.

It was a good thing Jane's house was big, for there were quite a lot of people in it. She had a papa and a mama, a sister, and six brothers. There were other boys who lived there, too—Papa's students. Papa had a school at home, where he taught the boys and his sons. He looked after the family's farm. And he was the rector: each Sunday he stood tall in the old gray church, telling everyone about God and His mysterious ways. He used long, complicated words that to Jane were almost like another language, strange and beautiful.

Papa worked hard. So did Mama. From dawn till dusk, in and out she went, in charge of the house and the garden, the children, the chickens, the cows, even the bees humming in their hives. And everywhere, it seemed, were boys, large and small, taking up a great deal of space. Where was Jane, amidst this bustle and clatter?

She watched and listened, thinking, learning. And playing, too, for she and the others had a lush green hill to roll down and a barn where they could go on rainy days. They had lanes to run along, pigs to visit at the farm, a pond to splash in.

Inside, in Papa's study, was a globe that spun and a microscope that made large the little wonders of the world, the *animalcules*, Papa called them. And there were books—not dozens, but hundreds of them—all lined up on the shelves, as if waiting, like secrets that wanted to be told.

In the evenings, in the parlor, Papa would read out loud. Here, in this one
dim room, into the mind's eye came the brave deeds of kings and the quick flash
of swords. There were funny clowns and sad lovers: tricks and jokes, tears and
battles. Wizards, monsters, fairies, fools; mountains, storms, ships crossing the
deep dark sea, soft beaches, and bright stars beyond counting.

As Jane came slowly to understand, even though
they all were gathered under the same roof, girls and
boys led very different lives. The boys had school
and lessons; they climbed trees and hunted and rode
horses—someday they would be gone, off to take
their place in the world as sailors, soldiers, lawyers,
landowners. But girls learned to sew and mend,
to sit up straight and be polite; they were to be *good*.

And Jane saw more: the shadow of poverty that fell hard upon the family. When she was seven, two new boys came—paying students for Papa.

They took the room she shared with Cassandra, her older sister. The girls were sent to the faraway house of Mrs. Cawley, who had a small, inexpensive school of her own.

It was so different. It wasn't *home*. Mrs. Cawley was cold, and the town
was noisy and dirty. Soon Mrs. Cawley took them to another town, which was
noisier and dirtier still. There, a terrible sickness caught hold of Jane.
It was hard to tell if she would live or die. Mama came hurrying to save
Jane and to bring her daughters home.

It took many months for Jane to get better. What could she do while everybody else was busy? She could read. Letters had become words, words had become sentences. Paragraphs became pages. Jane could read the books in Papa's study all by herself. So that is what she did. Shakespeare. Johnson. Cowper. Swift, Richardson, Defoe, and more. A dazzling universe opened up to her.

Somehow, Mama and Papa scraped together enough money to send
Jane and Cassandra to school again. This time it was the Abbey School for
young ladies where the pupils were taught a bit of spelling, penmanship,
and French; they had some lessons in music and dancing. These were the
things a girl should know. To be *ladylike*. To be a good wife. And in Jane's
world, getting married was the only thing a girl could hope for when she
grew up. A girl who didn't marry was odd. A failure. Maybe both.

There was Jane, nine years old, far from home. At the Abbey School were girls whose families had more money and were thought to be better, more important, than Jane's. These girls could look forward to glittering balls and beautiful gowns; they could dream of weddings and happily ever after.

Jane watched, listened, thought.

When Jane was ten, she and Cassandra came home. There was
no more money for school. Jane kept on reading; that was *her* school.
But now it wasn't enough to simply read. She came from a *writing* family:
Papa with his sermons, Mama with her funny poems, older brothers
who wrote and shared in the evenings to applause and laughter.

Jane decided to try it, too.

What would *she* write?

Her head was filled with bits and pieces of everything she had been reading. Perhaps she could start by rearranging what she already had.

So Jane began to write some little things. They were *like* the books she knew. But just as Mama—with her scraps of fabric and small, neat stitches—could turn an old gown into a new one, Jane found herself creating something new. Something different.

Were the girls in *her* stories sweet and obedient? Not at all! They were greedy and selfish and vain. Were her young men noble and wise? Oh, no! They were silly and foolish. Jane's characters—with names like Mrs. Kickabout, Pistoletta, Sir Edward Spangle, Old Humbug—behaved badly and did ridiculous things. There were places called Pammydiddle and Crankhumdunberry and Kilhoobery Park; there were cudgels and dungeons, fried cow's feet and stinking fish!

Jane's imagination soared like a wild bird. Her writing wasn't the least bit ladylike, but it was funny and clever. Her family laughed and clapped and laughed again. She wrote and wrote, getting better all the time.

One day, Jane met a handsome, intelligent young man. His name was Tom. Like Jane, he loved to laugh and to dance.

Jane liked him.

He liked Jane.

But they both were poor, and quickly Tom's family had him sent away.

Many girls Jane's age had already married, had homes of their own and children to care for. But not Jane. Tom was gone. And Jane was the girl who wrote. So she wrote a longer story. It was different from anything she had written before.

The heroine of "First Impressions" was a smart young lady named Elizabeth. She loved to laugh and dance, and came from a family that didn't have much money. One day she met a handsome, rich young man, Mr. Darcy. Some of his relatives and friends didn't approve of Elizabeth, but she proudly stood up for herself. And in the end Mr. Darcy, who feared he would lose Elizabeth forever, married her. They were to live happily ever after.

Jane's family loved "First Impressions."

They loved it so much that Papa even sent a letter to a publisher in far-off London. *Should you give any encouragement*, he wrote, *I will send you the work.*

It would be unladylike to publish a book, for that was something that mostly men did. But if it happened, Jane could know for sure she was a *real* writer. And she could earn money of her own.

The publisher said no.

What did Jane do then?
Life went on. She read, sewed,
planned menus for family meals;

she took long walks
and played the piano;

she went to parties
and visited relatives;
she helped take care
of her parents, she
helped take care of her
nieces and nephews.

And in between
all this, she kept on
writing her funny,
thoughtful stories.

When Jane was twenty-six, a young man named Harris asked her to marry him. Harris was so different from the Tom of long ago, but if she said yes, she could be like other women. And she would never have to worry about money again. She could live in a grand house, wear beautiful gowns, eat the most expensive foods.

Jane *did* say yes.

But the very next day, she told Harris that she had changed her mind. Years later, she would write: *Anything is to be preferred or endured rather than marrying without Affection.*

Hard times followed. Papa died: dear Papa, who with his steadfast love had encouraged Jane all her life. Now it was just Mama and Cassandra and Jane on their own. They moved, and moved again, always scrimping and contriving. Jane had worked hard on her stories, but nobody, it seemed, wanted to publish them.

Then came the news that one of Jane's brothers had a house where they could live.

Mama, Cassandra, and Jane settled down once more. And something wonderful happened. Jane's story about two sisters, called *Sense and Sensibility*, was published! At last, she was an *author*—with a book, filled with her words, that she could hold in her hands, turn its pages, place on a shelf.

Soon, Jane's story "First Impressions," now called *Pride and Prejudice*, was also published. When she received her first copy in the mail, she wrote joyfully to Cassandra: *I have got my own darling Child from London.*

People liked these two books so much, the publisher had to print more copies. Jane was earning money.

Two more of her stories were published:
Mansfield Park and *Emma*.

All over England, people were buying,
reading, and enjoying Jane's books. Even
the Prince Regent loved them. He had his
librarian go see Jane, and she was invited
to visit the palace!

It was like spring finally arriving after
a long, dark winter. Jane's dream of being
a writer and an author had come true.

She had more stories she wanted
to tell, other books she wanted to
share. A tale about a girl who liked
ghosts and mysterious castles. And
another story, more serious, about
a lady—not so young anymore—
who thought she had lost the love
of her life.

Jane kept writing.

But she began to feel unwell.
As the months went by, her health
worsened. The doctors could do
nothing to help her.

When she was forty-one years old, Jane died,
held close in the arms of her sister, Cassandra.
The two books, *Northanger Abbey* and *Persuasion*,
were published later that year.

Who would have thought, when Jane was a little girl, scribbling away in her tiny village, that one day the Prince Regent would admire her—would respect her talent? And who would have thought that two hundred years later, Jane would be one of the most beloved writers in the world?

Today, Jane's books can be found in just about every country, in many different languages, on shelves and on screens, and in people's hearts. Her words and ideas—her stories and her laughter— are everywhere.

THE LIFE AND TIMES OF
JANE AUSTEN

JANE AUSTEN lived from 1775 to 1817. Although she's one of the world's most popular authors, there's a lot we don't know about her, especially her childhood. Unlike many other writers, she didn't leave behind a diary or journal. She published her first four books without using her name. It wasn't till long after Jane's death that both she and her six books (and other work) got more and more recognition.

So how do we determine what Jane's life was like? Mainly through letters—some Jane herself wrote, others that mention Jane—and from what her family, friends, and acquaintances said after she died.

Not only was Jane a gifted writer,

she also presented the idea that a girl could use her intelligence to help her live the best life possible.

Back then, this was a bold notion. People thought very differently about what men and women could do. All too often, girls and women were viewed as less intelligent, less capable, less *interesting* than boys and men. Because of this thinking, the only "career" a girl could aspire to in Jane's world was marriage. Even that could be hard to achieve if she didn't have money given to her by her family.

Jane's family didn't have much money, but they *did* support her goal to become a published writer. At the time, that was bold, too. Most books were written by men. And the few women who published books often didn't use their real names, as that was considered unladylike—even shocking. Jane herself only had "By a Lady" printed as her byline in her first book, and "By the author of . . ." in the other three books published in her lifetime. (Although gradually her secret became known outside the family.)

What is even bolder is that Jane took on the financial risk of publishing three of those four books—a common arrangement at the time, with a publisher expecting writers to pay him back if a book didn't sell well. That Jane was willing to do this tells us a lot about how strongly she believed in herself and in her writing.

Once you know a little about Jane Austen, you can understand how unusual it was for a girl to want to be a writer. And how remarkable it was that she kept working hard—despite many setbacks—to become a published author. How courageous it was to turn down a marriage proposal that would have been the "correct" thing to do and would have freed her from endless money worries. And how daring, how brilliant it was to create a new kind of heroine in fiction: young women whom we still love to read about, talk about, laugh with, relate to, and admire today.

FROM THE PEN OF
JANE AUSTEN

NOT ONLY did Jane write books, she wrote many letters. Only a few remain today—mostly the ones saved by her sister, Cassandra—but they give us a glimpse of a strong, smart, playful person.

I will not say that your Mulberry trees are dead, but I am afraid they're not alive.

—to Cassandra after a powerful storm swept through their neighborhood

No—I must keep to my own style & go on in my own Way; And though I may never succeed again in that, I am convinced that I should totally fail in any other.

—to the Prince Regent's librarian, Mr. Clarke, who had suggested
that Jane write a book about the Prince's family

Handsome is as Handsome does; he is therefore a very ill-looking Man.

—to Cassandra

Jane also "spoke" through her stories and the things her characters say. Here are a few examples:

It is very unfair to judge of anybody's conduct, without
an intimate knowledge of their situation.

—from *Emma*, reminding us to not judge a book by its cover

They are much to be pitied who have not
been . . . given a taste for Nature in early life.

—from *Mansfield Park*

It is a truth universally acknowledged, that a single man in possession
of a good fortune must be in want of a wife.

—the famous first sentence from *Pride and Prejudice*, in which Jane pokes fun
at the idea of marriage being the most important thing in life

JANE'S ADMIRERS

OVER THE YEARS, many famous writers—from Rudyard Kipling and C. S. Lewis to Dodie Smith and Katherine Paterson—have had nice things to say about Jane Austen. Here are a few of them.

Jane Austen is the pinnacle to which all other authors aspire.

—J. K. ROWLING

She is not a gentle writer.

—FAY WELDON

A little aloof, a little inscrutable and mysterious, she will always remain, but serene and beautiful also because of her greatness as an artist.

—VIRGINIA WOOLF

She's as perfect in literature as Mozart is in music, and she gives me the same sort of feeling. But apart from that, she is the first of the great novelists.

—FRANK O'CONNOR

Now I am reading the divine Jane. I think she has much to teach me.

—SAMUEL BECKETT

LEARNING MORE ABOUT JANE AUSTEN

Two museums in England are dedicated to the life and work of Jane Austen.

- In the city of Bath, where Jane both visited and lived, is the JANE AUSTEN CENTRE, which offers exhibits, costumed staff who portray the people in Jane's stories, walking tours, a beautifully decorated tearoom, even a wax model of what Jane might have looked like.

- Located near the town of Alton, the house where Jane spent the last eight years of her life—called Chawton Cottage when she lived there—has become the JANE AUSTEN'S HOUSE MUSEUM, hosting a variety of exhibits, classes, and events. Nearby is Chawton House Library, formerly part of the estate of Jane's older brother Edward; it's now a world-renowned research and learning center for the study of women's writing from 1600 to 1830.

THE JANE AUSTEN SOCIETY was founded in 1940 in the United Kingdom to raise money for the preservation of Chawton Cottage and now promotes the enjoyment and study of Jane's work, her life, and her evolving literary influence. Today there are similar organizations all over the world, including North America, Australia, Brazil, and Japan.

THE JANE AUSTEN LITERACY FOUNDATION was established in 2014 by Caroline Jane Knight, a direct descendant of Jane Austen's brother Edward. It helps provide free literacy resources—including books and writing materials—for communities in need.

SOURCES

Becoming Jane Austen by Jon Spence, Hambledon Continuum, 2003

Jane Austen: A Life by David Nokes, Farrar, Straus and Giroux, 1997

Jane Austen: A Life by Carol Shields, Viking, 2001

Jane Austen: A Life by Claire Tomalin, Vintage, 1999

Jane Austen: Catharine and Other Writings, edited by Margaret Anne Doody and Douglas Murray, Oxford University Press, 1993

Jane Austen: Her Life by Park Honan, St. Martin's, 1987

Jane Austen the Woman: Some Biographical Insights by George Holbert Tucker, St. Martin's, 1994

Jane Austen's Letters, 4th edition, edited by Deirdre Le Faye, Oxford University Press, 2011